Teen ELI

The ELI Readers collection is a complete range of books and plays for readers of all ages, ranging from captivating contemporary stories to timeless classics. There are three series, each catering for a different age group; Young ELI Readers, Teen ELI Readers and Young Adult ELI Readers. The books are carefully edited and beautifully illustrated to capture the essence of the stories and plots. The readers are supplemented with 'Focus on' texts packed with background cultural information.

The FSC certification guarantees that the paper used in these publications comes from certified forests, promoting responsible forestry management worldwide.

For this series of ELI graded readers, we have planted 5000 new trees.

ANGELA TOMKINSON

FESTIVALS
are
FUN

A JOURNEY THROUGH BRITAIN'S FESTIVALS AND EVENTS

Teen ELi Readers

Festivals are fun
by Angela Tomkinson
Language Level Consultants: Lisa Suett

ELI Readers
Founder and Series Editors
Paola Accattoli, Grazia Ancillani, Daniele Garbuglia (Art Director)

Graphic Design
Airone Comunicazione – Sergio Elisei

Layout
Airone Comunicazione

Production Manager
Francesco Capitano

Photo acknowledgements
Shutterstock

© 2018 ELI s.r.l.
P.O. Box 6
62019 Recanati MC
Italy
T +39 071750701
F +39 071977851
info@elionline.com
www.elionline.com

Typeset in 12 / 15 pt Monotype Dante

Printed in Italy by Teconstampa Recanati – ERT260.01
ISBN 978-88-536-2402-4

First edition: March 2018

www.eligradedreaders.com

Contents

6	Animals
8	Birthdays
10	Customs
12	Dance
14	Entertainment
16	Fire
18	Green festivals
20	Heritage
22	Island festivals
24	Jorvik
26	Kids' festivals
28	Literature festivals
30	Music
32	Notting Hill
34	On new year's eve
36	Patron saints
38	The Queen
40	Races
42	Summer festivals
44	Transport festivals
46	Unusual festivals
48	Village festivals
50	Winter festivals
52	Xmas
54	Yummy things to eat
56	Zzzzz… the festival of sleep
58	Activities

These icons indicate the parts of the story that are recorded

start ▶ stop ■

▶ 2 In Britain people love animals. Many families own a pet such as a dog, cat or rabbit but also other unusual animals too. Every year different events take place to celebrate this love. Read on to find out more.

Do you know?

The Cocker Spaniel is the type of dog that has won the Best in the Show prize the most times.

Crufts

Do you know Crufts? It's the biggest dog show in the world and it's in the Guinness Book of World Records! A man called Charles Cruft started the first show in 1891. He worked as a manager for a dog biscuit factory. In the beginning there were about 2,000 dogs in the show. Now there are about 23,000! The dogs and their owners* can win different prizes but the most important is for the 'Best in the Show'.

The Royal Welsh Show

This is one of the biggest farmer's shows in Europe and is in July in Wales. The event started in 1904 and the 'Royal Welsh Agricultural Society' organised the first show. It lasts for four days and more than 200,000 people come to visit it. There are many different events during the show and there are prizes for the best farm animals such as cows, sheep, horses, goats and pigs. There are also sheep shearing competitions (taking the wool off the sheep) and a prize for the best sheepdog. You can also find some of the Royal family there who like visiting the show.

animals

Swan Upping

This unusual event first happened in the 12th century. Now it happens every year in July. A group of people called 'Swan Uppers', who wear red coats, have to catch and count the swans they find on the River Thames near London. Some of these swans belong to the Queen. In the past the swans became the food of the Royal banquets* but now they are counted and checked for health reasons. The swan uppers travel for about 79 miles along the River Thames and it usually takes them about five days to complete the census*.

Do you know?

Swans can fly as fast as 95km an hour and they have more than 25,000 feathers on their body.

Whittlesey Straw Bear Festival

This is a very old custom and is to do with an animal, but not a real one! This celebration* is on the first Monday after Twelfth Night (5th January). A man or boy from the village of Whittlesey in Cambridgeshire wears straw* all over his body to look like a bear. He dances his way around the village followed by the local people and musicians. At the end of the celebration the villagers burn the bear costume and there is music, dancing and eating.

Do you know?

44% of homes in Britain have a pet. Almost ¼ of them own a dog. The most popular names for British people's dogs last year were: Bella, Poppy and Alfie.

banquets an important dinner for many people
celebration a special day like a birthday
census a way of counting the number of a people in a country
owners people who possess something like a house or a shop
straw

birthdays

What's your favourite day of the year? Your birthday? And how do you celebrate an important birthday in your country? Would you like to have more than one birthday? Let's take a look at some interesting birthdays!

Eighteen at last!

In Britain an important birthday is usually your eighteenth. After this age you can vote, drink in a pub, get married without asking your parents and open a bank account. Teenagers often have a party with their friends and family and receive some very nice presents.

What do you usually do on your birthday?

Two birthdays

Did you know that Queen Elizabeth II has two birthdays? She has her 'real' birthday on April 21st when she celebrates together with her family. Then, she has her 'public' birthday in June which she celebrates with a parade*.

The Queen's 90th Birthday

In 2016 Queen Elizabeth had her 90th birthday. It was a big event at Windsor Castle. Actors, musicians and dancers told the story of her life and 900 horses were in the parade. There was also a very big street party with 10,000 guests near Buckingham Palace.

Birthday Cards

In Britain it's usual to send your friends or family a birthday card. These cards first became popular in the 1800s after the stamp was born and it became cheaper and easier to send cards by post. Today, many people prefer e-cards (electronic cards) on the Internet as they can add music and a photo to the card so it becomes more personal*. They're also cheap to send, easy to use and arrive in less than a second!

✻

In April 2017, Jack Reynolds from Manchester became the oldest person in the world to ride on a roller coaster* for the first time. He did this on his 105th birthday and broke a Guinness World Record. The year before, he became the oldest person in the world to have their first tattoo at the age of 104!

✻

Birthday Bumps

In Britain, children usually give each other the 'bumps' when it's their birthday. This means that two or more people pick you up by your arms and legs and lift* you up and down, one for each year of your age and then one more for good luck.

Do you know?

Happy Birthday to You is the most well-known song in English around the world. Today, people sing it also in many different languages.

lift carry someone so they don't touch the floor
parade a group of people that walk in a line so that people can look at them
personal made just for that person
roller coaster

9

▶ 4

When you think of Britain, what words and pictures come into your head? Do you think British people drink a lot of tea or do they prefer coffee? What do they like speaking about? And what's funny about British humour? Why do they enjoy standing in a line? Read on to learn about some of the answers to these questions.

Drinking Tea

People in Britain love drinking tea. Every day British people drink 165 million cups! This love for tea first started in the 18th century when travellers brought tea from India and China to Britain. Most British people like theirs dark and strong but with a lot of milk. Making a perfect cup of tea isn't so simple and in 1946 the English writer George Orwell even wrote an essay★ called "A Nice Cup of Tea" where he wrote down the eleven different rules★ for making a cup of tea.

★

In English we have a lot of phrases that speak about tea. For example, 'it's not my cup of tea' means you don't like something, it isn't for you. If you really don't want to do something, you can say 'I wouldn't do it for all the tea in China' and if you want to say someone or something is very British you can say 'as English as a cup of tea'.

★

The Weather

Many people think that British people speak a lot about the weather. This is actually true! This is because the weather changes a lot in Britain and it's possible to have four seasons in one day. But it's also a way to start speaking with someone that you don't know very well. For example, while you're waiting for the bus you can say to someone 'Cold today, isn't it?'. This isn't really a question as you already know the answer, but it's a way to make polite conversation.

customs

10

✱

In English there are also a lot of phrases about the weather and people try to understand what the weather will be like the next day. For example, some people say 'A ring around the sun or moon means that rain will come real soon' or 'Rain before seven, clear before eleven'. Do you have any similar phrases in your language?

✱

Queueing

British people spend a lot of time queueing, which means standing in a line and waiting for your turn*. This can be at the post office, at the supermarket or waiting for the bus. And never try to jump the queue in Britain. People will look at you in a bad way!

British Humour

Not everyone understands British humour, especially if they come from another country outside Britain. British people often make jokes about themselves and don't take themselves too seriously.

It's often difficult to understand if a British person is joking or not as they usually do it with a serious face. They often use humour to speak about everyday life and even when things go badly they sometimes make a joke about it.

✱

Popular British jokes are often about an English man, an Irish man and a Scottish man… Do you have similar jokes in your country?

✱

essay a short piece of writing on one subject
rules formal words to say what you must or mustn't do
turn the time when someone in a group should do something

dance

We can say that many British celebrations and events have dancing as an important part of them. Many different types of dances are fun to watch but also fun to do. Young people and old people take part and usually parents and grandparents teach their children the meaning and the importance of these dances. Are you ready to dance?

▶ 5 **Let's dance around the Maypole**

Do you know what a Maypole is? Well, it's a very tall pole* made of wood. It usually has long pieces of ribbon* on it which the dancers hold in their hands when they're dancing. About 10 boys and girls dance around the pole while music is playing. You can find these Maypoles in many towns and villages in Britain and they celebrate the start of Spring. During this dancing, sometimes they choose a young girl to be the May Queen and she wears a white dress with flowers in her hair.

Do you know?

People say that the tallest Maypole in history was put up on the Strand in London in 1661. It was more than 143 feet high. People also say that in 1717 the famous astronomer and scientist Isaac Newton used the pole to hold his new telescope. What do you think?

12

Morris dancing

This is another type of traditional folk dance. The dancers are often men who wear bells* on their legs and carry pieces of wood, swords* or handkerchiefs in their hands. There are normally 6 or 8 dancers in two lines or in a circle who stand in front of each other. This dance is very old and comes from the 15th century. Together with the dancers there are usually musicians who play a violin, a drum or an accordion. Sounds like fun?

✻

The Industrial Revolution started in Great Britain in 1760 and lasted until 1840 and is a very important event in world history. People changed from producing things by hand to producing things with machines.

✻

Clog dancing

Do you like making a lot of noise? Then this could be the dance for you! It's a traditional dance, especially from the north of England, and the dancers wear clogs on their feet (shoes made of wood). This dance first started in the 19th century during the Industrial Revolution and the people who worked in the cotton factories wore these shoes for work. During their breaks and lunchtime they had competitions to see who could make the best rhythm with their feet. This later became a dance and clog dancing competitions still take place today. One of the most important is the Lancashire and Cheshire Clog Dancing contest every September in the north of England.

Do you know?

The famous silent movie actor Charlie Chaplin started his career as a clog dancer before becoming an actor.

bells
pole a long thin piece of wood or metal
ribbon
swords

13

▶ 6   In Britain there are many festivals about entertainment. Awards* festivals for the best in music or film, magic festivals, light festivals … there's something for everybody.

The Brit Awards

These are pop music awards that are on every year in London. They're in May and the first one was in 1977. There are awards for many different things such as Best Album, Best Group, Best Singles, Best Male singer, Best Female singer… Robbie Williams has won the most Brit awards – 13 as a solo singer and 5 with the group *Take That*.

✻

The girl group *Little Mix* won the award for Best British Single last year at the Brit Awards. They became a group in 2011 when they met at *X Factor UK*. They sang very well together and they actually won *X Factor* that year!

✻

The BAFTA Awards

This is the British Academy Film Awards. They're in February every year and 2017 was the 70th anniversary. There are awards for many different things such as Best Film, Best Actor, Best Actress, Best Music in a film … Last year the film *La La Land* won the award for Best Film and Emma Stone for Best Actress.

14

Blackpool Magic Festival

Do you like magic? Would you like to be a magician? Then this festival could be for you! It started 64 years ago in Blackpool in the north west of England. It's in February and lasts four days. It's for anyone who likes magic – for professionals* and non-professionals and those who like magic as a hobby. In 2015, the festival won a Guinness Book of Records award for the biggest number of magicians in one place!

✳

Sometimes the magician *Dynamo* is also at the festival. Do you know him? His real name is Steven Frayne and he's from Bradford in the north of England. He has a TV show called *Dynamo: Magician Impossible*. In 2011, many people were surprised when they saw him on the River Thames in London – not in a boat, but walking on top of the water!

✳

Blackpool Illuminations

Blackpool, in the north west of England, is also famous for another festival – Blackpool Illuminations. This is a festival of light and the town is full of lights of all different colours. It first started in 1879 and the lights are on from the end of August until the beginning of December. There are more than 10km of lights and people call it 'the greatest light show on earth!' It takes 22 weeks to put up all the lights and 9 weeks to take them down! It's also a 'green' festival as they use renewable* energy for the lights, from the sun, the wind and the water.

awards a prize for doing something well
professionals people who do magic as a job
renewable something that can be used again

15

7 Britain is a land full of traditions and customs both ancient* and modern and many of them are to do with fire. Read on to find out more.

fire

*
Remember, remember!
The Fifth of November,
The Gunpowder treason and plot;
This is the beginning of a poem from 1870 that speaks about Guy Fawkes and what happened on November 5th. People still use this poem today. You can also hear it in the 2005 film *V for Vendetta* with Natalie Portman.
*

Bonfire Night (Guy Fawkes Night)

This takes place on November 5th every year and is hundreds of years old. In 1605 a group of 13 young men tried to blow up* the Houses of Parliament with the government and king inside. But they couldn't do it and a young man called Guy Fawkes was the only one who went to prison. After they heard the news many people built big fires because they were happy that the king was saved. Now families usually have a bonfire party in their garden or go to an organised one in the park, have fireworks* and eat special food.

Imbolc Fire Festival

This very old festival takes place in Huddersfield in the north of England at the beginning of February. It comes from a 2,000 year old Celtic festival that celebrated the arrival of Spring. During the festival there's a big parade with lanterns and torches with fire jugglers* and people who wear Celtic costumes. There are also two 12 feet high figures* – Jack Frost who represents Winter and the Green Man who represents Spring.

16

Burning the Clocks

This is a modern celebration and was born in 1993. It takes place in Brighton on December 21st in the south of England. The local* people make paper lanterns and wear costumes that have clocks on them. These clocks show the passing of time. They walk through the town to the sea and there is a big bonfire where they burn their lanterns and watch the firework show. This happens on the shortest day of the year.

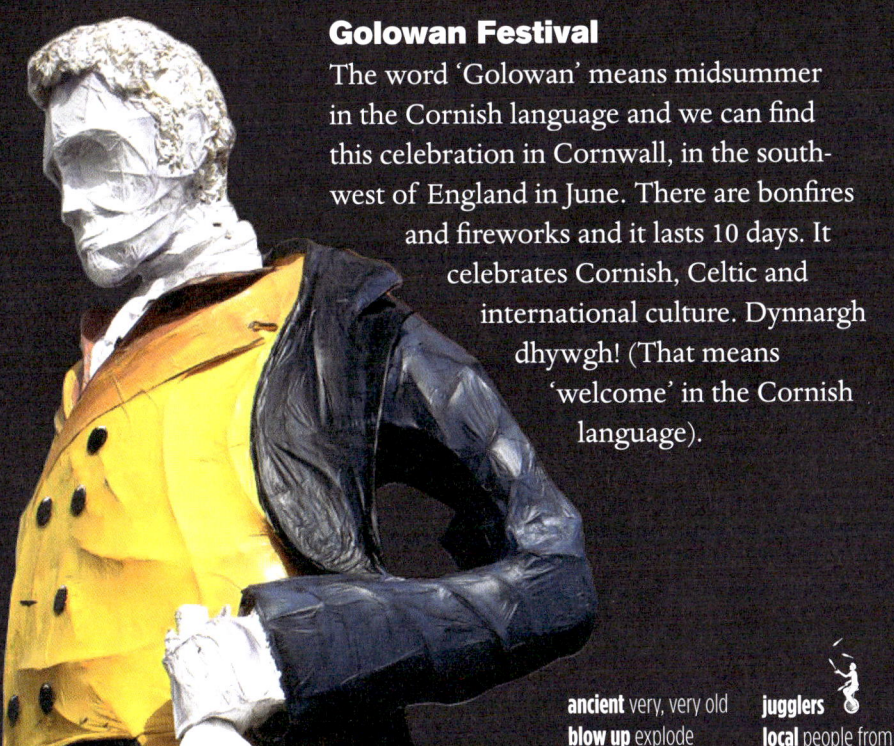

Golowan Festival

The word 'Golowan' means midsummer in the Cornish language and we can find this celebration in Cornwall, in the south-west of England in June. There are bonfires and fireworks and it lasts 10 days. It celebrates Cornish, Celtic and international culture. Dynnargh dhywgh! (That means 'welcome' in the Cornish language).

ancient very, very old
blow up explode
figures characters
fireworks
jugglers
local people from that place

17

green festivals

▶ 8

Chelsea Flower Show

Do you like plants and flowers? Then, you'll love this event. The Chelsea Flower Show happens in May every year and lasts 5 days. It first started in 1862 and is the biggest and most famous flower show in Britain. Many people from all over the world come to the show.

Green Man

This is a music and arts festival that you can find in mid-August in the Brecon Beacons in Wales. It lasts* four days and it includes music, literature, film, comedy, theatre and poetry. During the last festival there were 1,500 different performances on 17 different stages*. People love this festival not only for the music and other shows, but for the beautiful place where the festival is.

Britain is very green. It has many parks and gardens full of flowers and plants. When the weather is good, people like spending time outside in these places. During the year, there are many events and festivals where we can visit these parks and gardens and have fun in the fresh air.

18

Green Gathering

This is a festival that thinks about the environment*. It's in Wales on the first weekend of August. There's music, art and people that speak about 'green' things like saving the environment and being greener in our homes. The festival uses solar energy from the sun and wind energy to power everything.

Earthwise 888

You can visit this festival at the beginning of August near the Uffington White Horse in Oxfordshire. You can see this drawing of a big white horse on the hill near the village of Uffington. People think that it's very old and it maybe comes from the Iron Age (800BC - AD100). This festival is very green. There's music but also people that speak about how to help the environment and help animals too.

Eden Project

Don't be surprised if you go to Cornwall in the south-west of England and see two enormous domes*. This is the Eden project, home to thousands and thousands of plants from around the world. One dome is for plants from the rainforest and the other for plants from the Mediterranean. There's also a botanical garden outside. Every summer there are music concerts there and in the past singers like Amy Winehouse, Paolo Nutini, and Elton John sang at the Eden concerts.

Do you know?

They filmed a part of the 2002 James Bond film 'Die Another Day' at the Eden Project.

domes a round roof on a building
environment the natural world
lasts continues for some time
stages the place where musicians play during a concert

9   Britain is rich in history and has lots of very old and beautiful places to visit. Let's have a look at some of them together!

heritage

Forth Bridge

UNESCO World Heritage Sites

UNESCO (the United Nations Educational, Scientific and Cultural Organisation) decides which places in the world can have this special title. The places must be important for culture or nature. In Britain there are 26 World Heritage Sites – 16 in England, 5 in Scotland, one both in England and Scotland, 3 in Wales and 1 in Northern Ireland.

The Giant's Causeway, Northern Ireland

We can find this unusual place in County Antrim on the north coast of Northern Ireland. It became a World Heritage Site in 1986. People think the Giant's Causeway was born after a volcano* many many years ago but some people also believe that a giant* built this place. It's a group of tall stones that become smaller and smaller as they go into the sea. They are like steps that you can walk across. People also call this place the Giant's Eyes, the Giant's Boots and the Organ.

The Forth Bridge, Scotland

This is one of Scotland's UNESCO World Heritage Sites and is the symbol of Scotland. They started building it in 1882 and finished in 1890. It is 2,529 metres long and is made of steel*. About 4,600 men helped to build it and it was a very difficult job to do. For 28 years the bridge was the longest and then the second longest bridge in the world.

Do you know?

We can see the Forth Bridge on one pound coins and in a Grand Theft Auto computer game.

20

Hadrian's Wall, Northern England

This is a Roman wall that the Romans built in 122 A.D. They built it across the line between the Roman area of Britannia and the part that belonged to the Barbarians. At the time the emperor was Hadrian so the wall took his name. Today you can still see a big part of the wall that goes across the north of England.

The Castles of King Edward, Wales

One of Wale's World Heritage Sites is a group of four medieval castles in Gwynedd in Wales. They're Beaumaris, Conwy, Caernarfon and Harlech Castles. Edward I (1272-1307) built them to save his kingdom.*

✸

There are special days during the year called 'Heritage Days' when people can visit for free well-known places but also ones that aren't usually open to the public.

✸

Stonehenge, England

Probably England's most famous World Heritage Site is Stonehenge in Wiltshire. It's a circle of very tall stones and it's about four and a half thousand years old. People aren't very sure why it's there but there are many stories about it. Some people believe that the wizard Merlin brought the stones from Ireland. Many people believe that it was a temple*. However, we know that the stones are very big and very heavy so it was very difficult to carry them there! What do you think about it?

giant
kingdom a country with a king or a queen
steel a strong metal
temple
volcano

21

▶ 10 Of course, we all know that Britain is an island but did you know that there are more than 6,000 small islands in the British Isles? They all have their own traditions and festivals so let's read on to find out more!

island festivals

Tynwald Day

This takes place on the Isle of Man. We can find this island in the Irish Sea between England and Northern Ireland. On 5th July every year there's Tynwald Day which is their national day. Tynwald is the name for their local government and on this day the government meets outside the parliament on Tynwald Hill. The Manx people (people from the Isle of Man) can ask them things and say what they aren't happy with. On the same day there are also concerts, dances, markets and fireworks. Tynwald Day is a very old tradition and it was born more than 1,000 years ago.

Do you know?

The biggest island in Britain is Lewes in the Outer Hebrides in Scotland. It has an area of 2,179km.

Battle of Flowers

This carnival takes place every year in August in Jersey in the Channel Islands. These are a group of islands that are in the English Channel near the coast of France. It first started in 1902 to celebrate the day when Edward VII became king. The carnival lasts two days with music, fireworks and a parade of people and floats full of flowers. In the past people had a 'battle' with the flowers but not now. On the last night of the carnival there's a moonlight parade where there are lots of lights and fireworks. It's magic!

✽

Britain's Chief Scout is Bear Grylls, the British adventurer and TV presenter. His many TV shows include *Running Wild*, *Mission Survives*, *Get Out Alive* and *Man Vs Wild*. Do you know them?

✽

Brownsea Island

This is a small island in the port of Poole, in the south of England. At the start of the 20th century a rich man bought the island and important people such as the Italian inventor and engineer Guglielmo Marconi and Robert Baden-Powell, a British army officer came to stay with him. On the island Baden-Powell held a camp for young boys in 1907 and this was the start of the Boy Scout movement. Now every year on the island there's an Open Air Theatre where you can watch some of Shakespeare's many plays and a wildlife✶ festival where you can see some interesting animals and insects.

Eisteddfod

This word means festival in the Welsh language. It's an 8 day festival of music, literature and performance. It's a very old festival and first started in the 12th century. It takes place in different places in Wales. In 2017 the Eisteddfod was on Anglesey, an island off the north-west coast of Wales. And do you know that Prince William and Kate lived on Anglesey for 3 years when they got married and William worked as a RAF pilot?

✽

The place with the longest name in Britain is in Wales. It has an amazing 58 letters. But can you say it? LLANFAIRPWLLGWYNGYLLGOGERYCHWYRNDROBWLLLLANTYSILIOGOGOGOCH

✽

wildlife animals, birds and plants that live in a natural environment ■

23

▶ 11

Would you like to be a Viking for a day? You can do this and much more at the Jorvik Viking Festival in York. Take a look to find out more!

Jorvik Viking Festival

It's the biggest Viking festival in Europe. It takes place every year in February in the city of York in the north of England. The festival lasts one week and it celebrates the last Viking king, Eric Bloodaxe. It's similar to a very old Viking festival called *Jolablot*. During the festival you can visit the Viking market, eat Viking food, listen to Viking music and hear Viking stories. Many people wear Viking costumes and fight in a Viking battle*. On the last day of the festival there's a very big parade and you can also see Viking longships on the river.

The city of York

York is a very old city with a lot of history. It's almost 2,000 years old. The Romans built the town in 71AD and called it Eboracum. It became the most important town of the Roman empire in Britain. Many hundreds of years later the Vikings arrived in Britain and took control of the city of York in 866AD. During the time of the Vikings, York became a very important river port with many boats that carried goods* and materials* around Britain and other countries. But almost one hundred years later the Vikings lost their battle* and had to leave Britain.

Do you know?

Judi Dench, the actress who played M in many James Bond films was born in York!

jorvik

24

Jorvik Museum

In York we can also find a very important Viking museum, called the Jorvik Museum. In 1984 they decided to build a new shopping centre in York. Under the ground* they found a lot of things from the time of the Vikings like plates, dishes, jewellery and parts of buildings. They found more than 40,000 objects. So they decided to put all these objects into a museum. Inside the museum you can see how the Vikings lived together with typical smells and sounds of that time.

Would you like to visit this museum? What kind of museums do you have in your town?

_____
_____
_____

Would you like a cup of tea?

In the centre of York we can find 'Betty's Tea Rooms'. It's one of the many symbols* of the city. A man called Frederick Belmont opened the café in York in 1936 after he travelled on the Queen Mary ship. He thought the ship was wonderful and so he asked the people who built the ship to help him build a very elegant tea shop and so Betty's was born. You can't miss the shop - there's always a very long queue* outside!

❋

Do you remember Guy Fawkes? We saw him in the pages about fire festivals. Do you remember what he did? Well, he was born in York too! In 1570.

❋

battle a fight
goods things you can buy and sell
ground the floor
materials things that you can use to make or do something
queue a line of people
symbols an object that represents someone or something

kids' festivals

What about festivals for younger people? Britain is full of those too. There are many different events for kids and teenagers that are exciting and fun too. If you like sport, pop music, classical music, cinema or cooking – there's something for everybody!

Glasgow Youth film Festival

This film festival started in 2008 and happens every February in Glasgow in Scotland. It lasts 10 days. It's a festival for young people from 3-17 years old. There are also workshops* about the cinema and the kids can learn about making films. There are also some famous filmmakers and actors who speak at the festival.

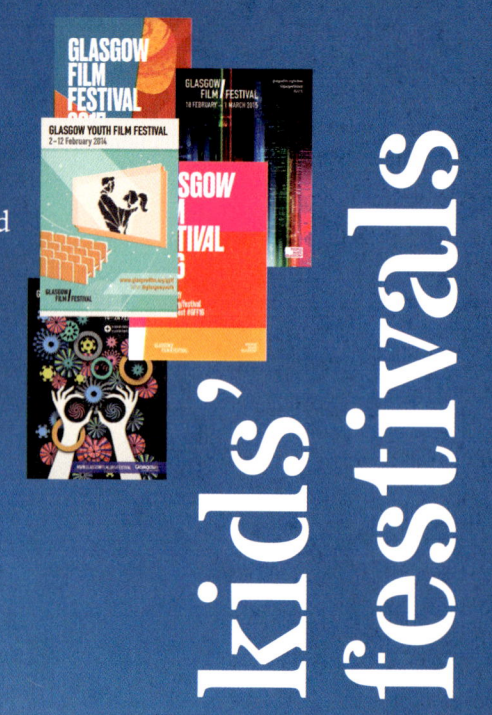

The Fold Out Festival

This is a new festival in Salisbury in the south of England. It's in April and it's for young people. During the festival, there's the Teenage Market where teenagers can sell some of their work such as art work, photographs, jewellery, clothes and food. Young people can also act or play music or sing on the stage.

Do you know?

Parkour was born in France in the 1980s. It's a sport that includes running, climbing and jumping around, across, through, under and over buildings and other places. People also call it Free Running. Would you like to try it?

Jersey Kids Triathlon

Do you remember something about Jersey? That it's in the Channel Islands in the English Channel? Well, here every year in June there's the sports event, the triathlon for children. The children are in different age groups and the oldest children have to swim 100 metres, ride a bicycle for 4.5 km and run 1,200 metres. Could you do that? The child who wins receives a special trophy* but actually every child in the triathlon is a winner!

✽

Alistair and Jonathan Brownlee are two brothers from Leeds, in the north of England. They both started doing the triathlon when they were children. Now they are Olympic medal winners. At the 2016 Rio Olympics Alistair won the gold medal and Jonathan won the silver.

✽

Music for Youth Festival

This is a five day music festival in July. It's in Birmingham in the centre of England. About 8,000 young musicians from Britain play different kinds of music during the festival. There are also dancers and singers as well as orchestras and small bands. Can you play an instrument?

trophy a big silver cup that the winner receives
workshops a kind of lesson where you can learn something

▶ 13 Many famous writers and poets come from Britain. How many do you know? Do you have a favourite? Here are some of the British festivals that celebrate these great artists.

Burns Night

Robert Burns was a well-known 18th century Scottish poet and every year on his birthday, 25th January, they organise celebrations in Scotland and Northern Ireland to remember him. The first celebrations took place in Scotland at the end of the 18th century and continue now. The celebrations can be formal or informal but there's always some Scottish food and drink such as haggis and Scotch whisky and the reading of Burns' poems.

Shakespeare

One of Britain's most famous writers is William Shakespeare. He was born in Stratford-Upon-Avon in central England. It isn't sure but people believe that he was born on April 23rd 1564 and died on April 23rd 1616. Every year on April 23rd the people of Stratford celebrate the life and the works of Shakespeare. There's a big parade in the town with music, dance, actors and the reading of his works. Children at school spend the day learning about him and studying some of his plays and poems.

Can you finish the names of his plays?
Romeo and _____
A Midsummer Night's _____
Twelfth _____
Winter's _____
King _____

literature festivals

Dickens

Charles Dickens is another famous English writer. He was born on 7th February 1812 and died on 9th June 1870. He spent a lot of his time in Rochester in the South of England and it was one of his favourite places. You can find the name of this place in many of his books. Every year in June the Dickens Festival takes place in this town with a parade, a fair, music, concerts and the reading of his books.

Can you finish the names of his books?
Oliver _____
David _____
A Christmas _____
A Tale of Two _____
Bleak _____

Dylan Thomas

Dylan Thomas is one of Wales's most important poets. He was born on 27th October 1914 in Swansea in Wales and died on 9th November 1953 at only 39 years old. For two weeks, from 27th October to 9th November, every year in Swansea there's the Dylan Thomas Festival. You can listen to some of his work and go to workshops and do different activities. Some of his most important works are the poem *Do not go gentle into that good night* and the play *Under Milk Wood*.

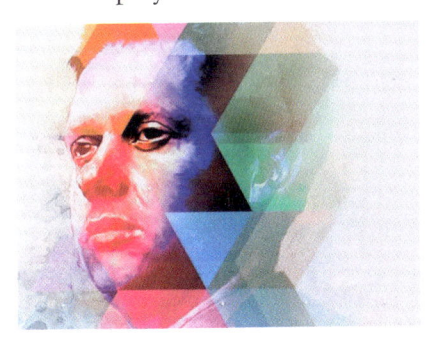

✱

There are many different films about the life and work of Dylan Thomas. The most recent films were in 2014 called *Set Fire to the Stars* with Elijah Wood (star of the Hobbit films) and 2016 *Dominion* with Rhys Ifans (who was in the film *Notting Hill*). ■

✱

British people love music! There are all kinds of music festivals – from pop to jazz, from hip hop to classical music. There's something for everyone!

Glastonbury

One of the most famous music festivals is in Glastonbury. It lasts five days and takes place the last week of June in Somerset in the south of England. It's a festival of modern music but also dance, theatre, comedy, circus and other artistic* things. It takes place in a big field and about 175,000 people go there. It first started in 1970. Many famous bands and singers play there.

Can you complete the Ed Sheeran song title? *Castle on the* _____

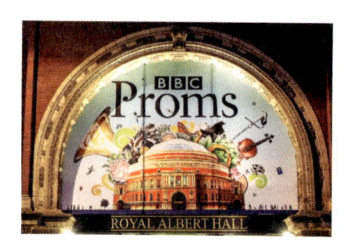

The Proms

This is a series of classical music concerts and lasts for 8 weeks. They take place at the Royal Albert Hall in London during the summer months. They first started in 1895 and the name comes from 'promenade concert' which were concerts outside in the parks and gardens of London. The most popular night is the Last Night of the Proms where they play very well-known, lively classical music and the audience* takes flags and balloons with them and sings with the music.

Can you complete the names of the royal couple? *Albert and* _____

music

The International North Wales Choral Festival

This is a singing competition that takes place every year at the beginning of November in Llandudno, in North Wales. It was born 28 years ago and choirs* from all over the world take part. In Wales people love singing and it's usually called the 'land of song'.

Can you complete the Coldplay song title? *A Head full of* _____

Do you know?

There's a music festival called the 'Underage Festival' in London where only teenagers can go. If you're older than 18 you can't enter!

Can you name any famous Welsh singers? _____

The Isle of Wight Festival

This very famous music festival was born in 1968 and continued for two years until 1970. Many great artists of that time played at the festival such as Jimi Hendrix, Miles Davis, The Doors, The Who, Leonard Cohen and many more. So many people went to the festival in 1970 that they decided to stop it as the Isle of Wight is a very small island! But in 2002 the festival started again and takes place every year. Many famous bands and singers such as the Rolling Stones, Amy Winehouse, Paolo Nutini, Paul McCartney, Coldplay, Kings of Leon, Queen, David Bowie… have played at the festival.

artistic something to do with art
audience people who go to listen to a concert
choirs a group of singers

notting hill

Do you know?
The rock band Pink Floyd played one of their first concerts as part of the carnival in 1966.

Notting Hill is an area in west London which is famous for the film with the same name but also for its very popular carnival. Do you want to learn more?

Let's enjoy the carnival
Notting Hill Carnival takes place every year in August. It first started in 1966 on the streets of Notting Hill. It's a carnival of Caribbean culture and it was started to unite* people of different races*. During the carnival there's dancing, music, eating and having fun!

Lots of numbers
People say that it's Europe's biggest street festival and that it's the second biggest carnival after Rio de Janeiro! It's actually as big as 11 Glastonbury music festivals! About 2 million people go and watch the carnival. There are about 15,000 different costumes in the parade and every costume is made by hand. The parade is 3.5 miles long and on the streets there are more than 300 food stalls* that sell Caribbean food. During the festival people eat 5 tons of chicken and one ton of rice and peas.

Film
Do you know the film *Notting Hill*? It's a romantic comedy and is from 1999. It stars Julia Roberts and Hugh Grant. The film won many awards and also a Brit Award for its music.

Notting Hill online
The carnival is becoming digital. You can download an app for your mobile that tells you all about the carnival. And in 2013 a video of some policemen dancing at the carnival went viral. It had 1.1 million hits* on YouTube.

Notting Hill Today
Today Notting Hill is a rich area where also famous people such as the singer Robbie Williams, chef Jamie Oliver and Fashion designer Stella McCartney like living. In this area we can find the famous Portobello Road Market and the lovely Kensington Gardens.

✻

The famous writer George Orwell (1984, Animal Farm) lived on Portobello Road for some time in 1927. And for film lovers, you can also see the area of Notting Hill in the films *Paddington* and *Bridget Jone's Diary*.

✻

A better life
In the 1950s and 1960s many people came from the West Indies to start a new life. The West Indies is a group of more than 20 islands in the Caribbean Sea with countries like Jamaica and Trinidad. The people came to look for a better life for their families. After the Second World War there weren't enough men to do a lot of jobs like bus drivers, postmen and work in hospitals, so they looked for people from the British colonies. But it wasn't very easy for them. Many West Indian families went to live in poor areas especially in London and Notting Hill was one of them.

hits visitors to a website
races groups of people who have the same language, culture....
stalls the place where you can buy and sell things in a market
unite join together

▶ 16 For many people the last day of the year is a very special event. They have parties, watch fireworks and think about the coming year. Different parts of Britain also do their own special things to welcome the new year. Let's take a look together!

Auld Lang Syne

When midnight arrives, people all around Britain cross their arms and join hands with people next to them. They sing a song called *Auld Lang Syne* which means 'times gone by' or 'past times'. Robert Burns, the Scottish poet, wrote the words to it in the 1700s. The song remembers old and new friends.

New Year Resolutions

At the end of the year many people in Britain make a resolution, this is a kind of promise to themselves to change something about their life in the new year. Many people make these 'resolutions' but find it hard to keep them!

> Do you ever make New Year resolutions? Do you usually keep them or do you sometimes break them?
> _____
> _____

on new year's eve

34

White Rabbits

Do you like rabbits? Well, in Yorkshire, in the north of England, people usually say 'Black rabbits, black rabbits, black rabbits' just before midnight on New Year's Eve. Then just after midnight they say 'White rabbits, white rabbits, white rabbits'. People think it brings good luck for the coming year.

Hogmanay

In Scotland they have Hogmanay on Dec 31st. The word comes from a kind of cake that children ate.

Calennig

In Wales, Welsh people often give each other an apple with dried fruit and a special leaf on it on New Year's Day. This brings them good luck during the year. On the same day, Welsh children often visit their neighbours and sing songs for them. Their neighbours usually give them cakes, apples, sweets and coins* for their singing.

New Year's Day Parade

For people who aren't feeling so tired after New Year's Eve, in the centre of London there's the New Year's Day parade. It first happened in 1967 and about a million people come to watch it on the streets of London. The parade is 3.2 km long and includes 8,500 cheerleaders, musicians, artists and dancers from around the world.

coins money

35

▶ 17   A patron saint is a saint that protects* a place or a person. In Britain we have four of them. Let's read all about them!

patron saints

Saint David

Saint David is the patron saint of Wales and we celebrate his day on March 1st. He was born in south west Wales in 589AD. Many places in Wales like Cardiff, Swansea and Aberystwyth have parades in the centre of the cities. Welsh people eat Welsh food such as *cawl*, a type of soup and *bara brith*, a type of bread. They also wear a leek (a long green vegetable) or a daffodil (a yellow flower) which are the traditional symbols of Wales. And did you know that in Disneyland Paris they also celebrate Saint David's Day? They have a week of Welsh events with fireworks and Disney characters who wear traditional Welsh clothes during the first week of March.

Saint George

Saint George is the patron saint of England and we celebrate his day on April 23rd. He became the patron saint of England in 1348, although he wasn't born in England, but in Turkey. There are many stories about him and people say that he killed a dragon and saved a princess. In the past, Saint George's day was as important as Christmas but now people have to go to work and children go to school in England on this day. But many English people think that this day should be a holiday. On this day many people wear a red rose which is England's national flower. In Trafalgar Square in the centre of London there's a concert to celebrate Saint George's day.

Do you know?

Scotland, Wales and Ireland all have their traditional Celtic languages. 19% of Welsh people can speak Welsh while 94,000 people use Irish every day. If you want to ask someone 'how are you?' in Welsh, you say: 'Sut wyt ti?' In Scottish Gaelic 'Ciamar a tha thu?' and in Irish Gaelic 'Conas atá tú?'

Saint Patrick

Saint Patrick is the patron saint of Ireland (the Republic of Ireland and Northern Ireland) and we celebrate his day on March 17th. He was born in Roman Britain in 385AD and Irish people all over the world celebrate his special day. One of the biggest Saint Patrick's Day parades is in New York with about 150,000 people in the parade and about 2 million people watching it on the streets of New York. The parade goes along 5th Avenue in Manhattan and lasts 5 hours. In Belfast in Northern Ireland, there's also a big carnival parade and music concerts. Irish people on this day wear green clothes and wear a shamrock (a green leaf).

St Andrew's Day

Saint Andrew is the patron saint of Scotland and we celebrate his day on November 30th. He became the patron of Scotland when Malcolm III of Scotland was king (1034-1093). On this day people celebrate Scottish culture with traditional Scottish food, music and dancing. Other activities that you can usually find on this day are art shows, storytelling, reading and writing poetry, cooking traditional Scottish dishes and bagpipe playing. In 2006 the Scottish Parliament decided to make this day a holiday so on this day schools and businesses are closed.

protects takes care of, looks after

the Queen

Name: Elizabeth Alexandra Mary Windsor
Born: 21st April 1926
Married to: Philip Duke of Edinburgh
Children: Charles, Anne, Andrew, Edward
Grandchildren: 8
Became Queen: 6th February 1952

Royal Garden Parties

Do you like going to parties? Would you like to go to the Queen's party? Every year she has some parties in the beautiful gardens of Buckingham Palace or the Palace of Holyroodhouse in Edinburgh in Scotland. The guests at the party aren't her family or friends, but people who do important things in their life to help others. At every garden party the guests usually eat 20,000 sandwiches, eat 20,000 pieces of cake and drink 27,000 cups of tea!

✻

Buckingham Palace has 600 rooms, 19 State rooms, 52 bedrooms, 78 bathrooms, 92 offices, a cinema and a swimming pool. It also has a post-office and a police station inside!

✻

Commonwealth Day

Do you know what the Commonwealth is? It's a group of 52 states, many of which were British colonies in the past, such as Canada, Australia, New Zealand, South Africa… Queen Elizabeth II is the Head of the Commonwealth. Every year on the 2nd Monday in March there's Commonwealth Day. There's a special event in Westminster Abbey which the Queen goes to. Every four years there's the Commonwealth Games, a kind of Olympic Games, for the countries of the Commonwealth.

Trooping the Colour

This event is also called the Queen's Birthday Parade. It happens in June to celebrate the Queen's 2nd birthday. Her real birthday is on April 21st but she also has an 'official' birthday on the second Saturday of June.

There's a parade that goes from Buckingham Palace down the Mall. The Queen sits in her carriage* during the parade. After she returns to Buckingham Palace and joins her family on the balcony. Together they watch the aeroplanes of the Royal Air Force that fly past to say 'Happy Birthday' to the Queen.

The State Opening of Parliament

This is a very old tradition and happens in May or June. The parliament usually meets in the Houses of Parliament in the centre of London. On this day, the Queen goes to the Parliament and sits on a special throne*. She sends a person called her 'Black Rod' to give a message to the politicians of the parliament who are waiting in another room. The politicians (the MPs) only let the Black Rod enter the room if he knocks* on the door with his stick*. The government gives their plans for the year to the Queen and she reads this to everyone.

Do you know?

The Queen's father was King George VI. There was a film about him in 2010 with Colin Firth called *The King's Speech*. Have you seen it?

carriage
knocks hit your hand on something many times
stick a long thin piece of wood
throne

▶ 19 Britain has lots of different kinds of races. If you like watching or taking part, there's a race for everyone.
So what are you waiting for? Start racing now!

Oxford/Cambridge boat race

It takes place every year on the River Thames in London. It's a boat race between Oxford and Cambridge University boat clubs and the race is 6.8km long. The two teams are called Blues. The Oxford team wears dark blue while the Cambridge team wears light blue. The race first started in 1829. Until now Cambridge has won the race 82 times while Oxford has won it 80 times. But in 1877 it was a draw*! People say that the judge* fell asleep under a tree and didn't see which team won the race!

Have you ever been on a boat?
_____
_____

The Tour of Britain

Do you like cycling? Well, this sports event could be the one for you! It's a cycle race that takes place at different places all over Britain and lasts a number of days. There are 8 different stages* and the race is 1308.5km long. The race began just after World War Two and the winner of the race is the cyclist that finishes in the fastest time. The race goes through many cities but also through the countryside where cyclists have to ride up and down hills.

races

40

Brecon Beacons Ultra marathon

The Brecon Beacons is a national park in Wales. Some of the park is normally used for military training. The marathon is 46 miles long and goes across roads, canals, rocks and hills. It's a difficult race as it takes place in mid-November when the weather is very cold or there's even snow. All different kinds of runners from World Champions to normal well-trained runners take part. If you have a dog, you can even take it with you! You have 16 hours to finish the race so start running now!

Do you like running?
_____
_____

Have you ever been on a horse?
_____

Royal Ascot

This is one of the most important events in the British social calendar. It takes place every June on the Royal Ascot racecourse which is in Berkshire in the south of England. The first race took place in 1711 and Queen Anne was there at the event. And still today it's a royal event. Queen Elizabeth II and other members of the royal family usually go to watch the races. There are different horse races over the five days and the winners of each race win big prize money. It's also fun to see what people are wearing. Many women wear enormous hats!

Do you know?

Ascot racecourse is famous also at the cinema! For example, we can see the place in two James Bond films - *A View to a Kill* (1985) and *Skyfall* (2012).

draw when no team wins
judge the person who decides who wins the race
stages parts

41

Summer is a time for having fun and spending time with friends. The sun shines, school is over and the holidays are finally here. We spend more time outside and enjoy going to parks or to the beach. There are also many festivals and events we can go to, so let's read on to find out more!

Wimbledon

Summer means Wimbledon. It's the oldest tennis competition in the world and started in 1877. It's usually in late June and early July for two weeks. Many tennis fans go and watch the matches but also many people watch it on TV. There are five main events – Gentlemen's singles, Ladies' singles, Gentlemen's Doubles, Ladies' Doubles and Mixed Doubles. There are many traditions at Wimbledon and one of these is eating strawberries and cream at the event!

Summer Solstice

This is also called Midsummer and it happens on June 21st, the longest day of the year. For the summer solstice thousands of people go to Stonehenge where they wait for the sun to rise*. Some people wear unusual clothes and put flowers in their hair. They spend their time dancing and playing music, while they wait for the sun to arrive.

summer festivals

Ice Cream Festival

Summer also means ice cream. All around Britain in the summer months there are ice cream festivals. One of these is at Old Spitalfields Market in London. It's in June and lasts 3 days. 16 different ice-cream makers are in the competition to see who makes the best ice cream. The winner then goes to the European Ice Cream Championships.

What's your favourite kind of ice cream?

Where do you usually spend your holiday?

Summer Holidays

People often think that the weather is awful in Britain and that it always rains. This isn't true. The summer months can be warm and sunny and this is the time when many people go on their holidays to the beach. There are many different sea places in Britain where you can have fun and enjoy yourself. Some holiday traditions are walking on the pier (a long promenade that goes out into the sea), eating 'rock' (a long hard stick that's sweet), fish and chips and as much ice cream as possible!

Do you know?

It was Carlo Gatti, a Swiss Italian, who first brought ice cream to Britain. It was in 1851 and he sold the ice cream from his house in Kings Cross in London.

✳

15th July is St Swithin's Day. In Britain people say 'If it rains on St Swithin's Day, it will rain continuously* for 40 days. And if it doesn't, there will be clear skies for 40 days'. Do you think it's true?

✳

continuously without stopping
rise go up

43

transport festivals

Do you have a favourite type of transport? Car, plane, train? Well, you can find all of these and much more at different festivals in Britain during the year. Let's have a look!

The British Grand Prix

Do you like fast cars? Well, then this is the place for you! It takes place at Silverstone race track in Northamptonshire in the centre of England. It's one of the oldest Formula One races in the world and first took place in 1926. A man called Henry Segrave brought the race to Britain after winning the French Grand Prix in 1923. To finish the race you need to do 306.291km by going round the track* 52 times. And do you know which team has won the British Grand Prix the most times? Here's a clue – their cars are red and come from Italy. Yes! Ferrari, of course!

London to Brighton

Or if you prefer slow cars, then this is for you! The London to Brighton Veteran Car Run takes place the first Sunday of November. It's a very old event and started in 1896. All the cars that take part are very old too. They were built before 1905 so more than a hundred years ago. The race starts very early in the morning in Hyde Park in London. The cars go very slowly and they can't go faster than 32km an hour. The race finishes in Brighton, 87km away, and all the cars that arrive before 4.30pm win a medal*. Some famous people take part in the race and in 1971 Queen Elizabeth II took part!

Volkswagen camper vans

This is one of the biggest Volkswagen festivals in the world! It takes place in May in Cornwall in the south of England. The most important event is the parade of Volkswagen cars and vans and usually about 1,000 take part. The festival lasts 3 days and there's music, food and lots of fun. VW camper vans were very popular in the 1960s and 70s and are still popular today.
And do you know that famous chef Jamie Oliver travelled round Italy in a VW camper van for his TV programme *Great Escape*?

Duxford Air Festival

If you like going really fast, then this is the festival for you. At Duxford airfield in Cambridgeshire you can watch many different kinds of air shows. Here you can also find the Imperial War Museum, Britain's biggest air museum. There are more than 200 aeroplanes in the museum and also cars and boats used by the army*. During the summer months there are different air shows such as the Duxford Airshow where you can see very old planes but also modern ones in the sky. There's also the Flying Legends Airshow where you can watch many planes from the Second World War.

Hot Air Balloons

But if you prefer an unusual type of transport then this could be for you! Bristol International Balloon Fiesta takes place in August in south-west England and started in 1979. People come from all over the world to take part and in 2014 the fiesta broke a Guinness World Record when 90 balloons landed* in the same field!

army
landed when an aeroplane arrives on the ground
medal a small flat piece of metal given to a winner
track a piece of ground in a circle used for running

45

There are many unusual festivals in Britain. Some are very old and come from history while others are more modern. Read on to find out more!

The World Coal Carrying Championship

Do you know what coal is? Well, it's a kind of black rock that when people burn it, it makes energy. On Easter Monday in the village of Gawthorpe in north England there's a very unusual race. All the men from the village have to carry 50kg of coal for almost 1km and the fastest person is the winner. The record is 4 minutes and 6 seconds. Now there's also a women's race but they only have to carry 10kg!

The Cooper's Hill Cheese Rolling

This unusual event takes place in May near Gloucester in the centre of England. This race needs a big cheese and a hill. The cheese starts first and rolls down* the hill very fast. The people start running and try to catch the cheese. They have to run very fast and because it's a hill, they often fall and sometimes hurt themselves. The cheese often goes at 100km an hour and the first person to arrive at the bottom of the hill, wins the cheese!

Do you know?

There are more than 2,000 different kinds of cheese in the world and people think that the first cheese was made more than 7,000 years ago!

unusual festivals

Toe wrestling Championship

Maybe you do wrestling or even arm wrestling, but toe wrestling? This strange event takes place in Staffordshire and started in 1974. A group of friends weren't happy that Britain didn't win very much in the Olympic Games so they decided to start their own sport. All you need to take part is your feet without any shoes or socks on!

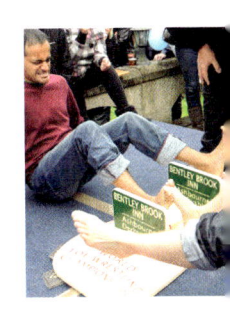

Hurling the Silver Ball

This event started more than 1,000 years ago and takes place in St.Ives in Cornwall. It's similar to a game of rugby. The mayor* of the town throws the silver ball to the group of local people who are waiting in the town square. They run through the streets of the town and try to take the ball from the person who is carrying it. The winner is the person who returns the ball to the mayor who is waiting at the town hall.

frying pan

Lent the period of 40 days before Easter
mayor the head of the city council
rolls down turns over and over

Great Spitalfields Pancake race

In Britain Shrove Tuesday is the last day you can eat 'fat' before the days of Lent*. This day is also called 'Pancake Day' as we eat pancakes on this day. In some towns and cities people take part in pancake races. A famous one is the Great Spitalfields race in London. People wear costumes and run down the street with a frying pan*. They have to throw the pancake in the air, catch it as many times as possible and run at the same time. Easy or not?

47

▶ 23

Britain is full of lovely villages. The people in the villages join together at festival time and work together to organise* some of these interesting and fun events. Let's take a look!

The Tolpuddle Martyrs' Festival

This takes places every year in Tolpuddle in Dorset. It's a festival that remembers a group of men who lived in this village in the 1830s. They all worked on farms but it was very hard and they didn't earn a lot of money. They decided to join together to make a group that fought for the rights of workers. However, the government wasn't very happy with this and sent them to prison in Australia. The English people fought against this decision. This festival is a celebration of them and the village remembers them every year.

Over to you

What about your town or village? Do you have any similar festivals?

Well-dressing

This is a summer event that happens in many villages in England. It includes decorating wells*, springs* or other types of water sources with pictures made from flower petals. It probably started as a pagan custom to say thank you to the gods for the water that arrived in the towns and villages. Tissington, a village in Derbyshire, was probably the first village in the UK to use again the custom in 1349, after the village escaped the Black Death* that killed many people at that time. Well-dressing isn't easy as you need 7 days to finish it and it usually lasts about a week.

village festivals

Tichborne Dole

This happens every year on March 25th in the village of Tichborne, in Hampshire in the south of England. It's a festival of charity and it started in the 12th century. Before she died Lady Mabella Tichborne told her family that she wanted them to give the poor people of the village food from the farm every year. Today the priest of the village gives bags of flour to the people in the village.

Over to you
What about your town or village? Does it help the poor people in some way? _____
_____

Rushbearing Ceremonies

In the Middle Ages nobody had carpets on the floor of their houses. They covered the floors with rushes*. Many villages at that time had special festivals when it was time to take the rushes from the fields. They made sculptures* with the rushes and carried them through the village in a parade. They tried to make better and bigger sculptures than the other villages near them. In some villages in the north of England this festival still takes place during the summer months. There's also music and singing during the parade.

Over to you
What about your town or village? Does it try to do something better or bigger than other villages near yours?
_____
_____

Black Death an illness that many people died from in the 1330s
organise plan and programme an event
rushes a type of tall grass that grows near water
sculptures 
springs a place where water comes from under the ground
wells a deep hole in the ground where you can take water

49

winter festivals

Winter is often cold, rainy and windy in Britain so many people prefer to stay inside at home. But just like the other months of the year, there are interesting and important events and festivals to visit. You can put on a warm coat and a scarf and forget about the bad weather. You'll certainly enjoy yourself!

The Lord Mayor's Show

Every year the City of London has a new Lord Mayor and this is an event to welcome him or her. It's on the second Saturday in November and includes a five-kilometre parade around the streets of the City. In 2015 it was the 800th anniversary so it's a very old event. The new Lord Mayor travels along the parade in a wonderful golden* carriage which is very different from the past when the Lord Mayor travelled by boat on the river or even on a horse.

Remembrance Sunday

This is on the second Sunday in November and is a day to remember all the people that died in World War I and II. On this day there are special events all over Britain and the biggest one is in London. The Royal family go there and people put wreaths* made of poppies* on war monuments. At 11a.m. everyone is silent for 2 minutes. Military bands play during the celebration and there are also big parades.

Do you know?

The coldest it has ever been in Britain was in Braemar in the Scottish Highlands. It reached -27.2° degrees!

Halloween

Today Halloween is popular all over the world but people think that it comes from a very old Celtic holiday called 'Samhain'. November 1st was the start of the Celtic new Year so people believe that October 31st celebrated the start of Winter. Now it's a festival for children who love wearing Halloween costumes and playing special Halloween games. They also go from house to house 'trick or treating' where they receive sweets and sometimes money from their neighbours.

Another unusual match is in the Orkney Islands off the coast of Scotland. Hundreds of men from the town are in two teams - the Uppies and the Doonies - and they have to try to catch the ball and put it in the goal at the other side of the town. Would you like to play?

Unusual football matches

During the winter months you can see some unusual football matches. One of these is in Scarborough on the north-east coast of England. It's a match between the fishermen and the firemen of the town. It's a very old custom and started in 1893. They played the first match to make money for the families of four fisherman lost at sea.

golden made of gold
poppies
wreaths a circle of flowers you give to the family of someone who is dead

51

▶ 25 December is a month full of magic. It's the month of Christmas, special family traditions and spending time together. We open presents, cook special food and wait for the snow to fall. We love Christmas!

Let's turn on the lights

One important tradition that happens at the beginning of Christmas time is the turning on of Christmas lights in many towns and cities across Britain. This usually happens at the end of November or the beginning of December. Especially in London this is an important event and there's also a concert with famous people who turn on the lights.

*

On Christmas Eve, December 24th, children in Britain put up a stocking, a kind of big sock, that they can fill with presents. They usually leave some food and drink out for Father Christmas and Rudolph, his reindeer.

*

A big tree

Another Christmas tradition is the turning on the lights of the Christmas tree in Trafalgar Square. The tree arrives every year from Norway and is a present from the Norwegian people as a thank you for Britain helping them in the Second World War. This tradition started in 1947 and is a symbol of peace and friendship. People often sing Christmas songs around the tree and it stays there until January 6th.

xmas

52

Too much food?

If you eat too much at Christmas and you need to do some kind of sport, well there are lots to choose from during this time. In the month of December at Battersea Park in London there's the 'Santa Run'. It's a 5km race where everyone wears a Father Christmas costume and either* walks, jogs or runs as fast or as slowly as they like. If you don't like running but prefer swimming, then you can swim in the sea or lake with other people who do it as a tradition. One place you can do this is in the Serpentine Lake in Hyde Park in London. The only problem is that it's usually freezing* at this time of year so don't be surprised if you feel a little cold in the water!

Boxing Day

The day after Christmas, December 26th, is called Boxing Day or St Stephen's Day. Many people in Britain like going shopping on this day as it's the first day of the sales*. Some shops open as early as 5a.m. and you can see very long queues outside some of them. Everybody wants to find something for a very good price and spend some of the money they received for Christmas. What do you usually do on the day after Christmas?

Stir-Up Sunday

This usually happens on the fourth Sunday before Christmas. In the past families were together in the kitchen and helped to make the traditional Christmas Pudding. The pudding is made with many different things such as eggs, flour, spices and dried fruit and everyone in the family stirred* the ingredients while making a wish*. Some families also put some money inside the pudding and the person who found it on Christmas Day would be lucky all year.

either one or the other of two
freezing very, very cold
sales a time when shops sell things at a lower price than usual
stirred move a liquid round and round with a spoon
wish say to yourself what you would like to happen

53

CHILLI FESTIVAL

yummy things to eat

🔊 26 The Hottest Festival in Britain

Do you like eating hot food? Then this is the festival for you! It's the Great Dorset Chilli Festival and it takes place every August in Dorset in the south of England. Here you can find many different dishes that use chilli especially the Dorset Naga, one of the world's hottest chillis that comes from Dorset. You can also learn how to grow your own chilli peppers. If chillis aren't a problem for you then you can also try the chilli jam and even the chilli chocolate! Yum yum! There's also a competition to see who can eat the hottest chilli! If chillis aren't for you, then you can listen to the music and visit the gardens and the 400 year-old house where the festival takes place. And why not try the Jamaican, Mexican, Thai and Indian street food?

Rhubarb Festival

Do you know rhubarb? It's a plant that has big green leaves and you can only eat it after cooking it. You usually find it in pies and desserts. In the north of England you can find the Rhubarb Triangle (Wakefield - Leeds - Morley) which is an area where rhubarb started growing 150 years ago. During the month of February you can go to the Wakefield Rhubarb Festival. There are lots of things to do there that include rhubarb. You can also learn how to use rhubarb in your cooking. Would you like to try?

Many festivals in Britain are about food and drink. You can try lots of different and unusual kinds of food, not only from Britain but also the rest of the world. Are you feeling hungry? What would you like to eat?

The Isle of Wight Garlic Festival

Not everyone likes garlic but here you can try something different from the usual food festival. There are more than 250 stalls that sell food with garlic in it and you can even try garlic seafood and garlic ice-cream. If you don't like garlic, then you can go and listen to the concert or visit the fun fair.

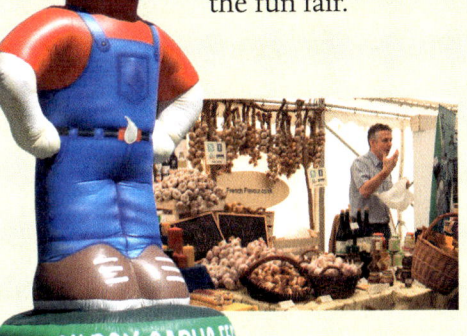

The Big Festival

Do you know the famous chef Jamie Oliver? Well, for 3 days at the end of August there's the Big Festival that takes place on a farm in the Cotswolds in south central England. Together with some other famous chefs he organizes this festival to make money for the Jamie Oliver's Better Food Foundation which helps poor or disabled* people. There are cooking shows, cooking lessons, lots of yummy food to eat and lots of fun things to do for kids.

Legenderry Food Festival

This 3-day festival takes place in Derry in northern Ireland. You can try lots of local food from the area such as oysters and goat burgers. It takes place 17th - 19th March during the St Patrick's Day spring carnival so everyone is ready to have fun. There's also music, cooking lessons and lots of things to do for kids.

disabled not able to use a part of the body because of illness

🔊 27

ZZZZZ... the festival of sleep

Do you like sleeping? How many hours do you usually sleep every night? Do you know how important it is to sleep well? What do you think happens at the Festival of Sleep? Let's have a look together!

Do you know?
We spend 1/3 of our life sleeping!

Music and Sleep
In 2015 British composer* Max Richter wrote some classical music called 'Sleep'. He played the music to a group of people at a concert and it lasted 8 hours. The people who listened to his music didn't sit on chairs, but in beds! They could go to sleep if they wanted to. His music is also a Guinness World Record for the longest single piece of music at a concert.

The Festival of Sleep
January 3rd is Festival of Sleep day in the UK but also around the world! What can you do on this day? Sleep, of course! Wear your favourite pyjamas, get into your bed and sleep for as many hours as you want! Probably they chose January 3rd as it's a few days after Christmas and New Year so people are tired and need to rest.

Sleeping in the afternoon
Sometimes people like sleeping in the afternoon after lunch for a short time. In some countries they call this *a siesta*, but in Britain you can also call it *a snooze, a nap, forty winks* and *grab some Zs*!

56

A night at the museum

At the Natural History Museum in London it's possible to spend the night there. Would you like to spend a night sleeping near a big dinosaur? Once a month your dream can become true! The event starts early in the evening with different activities about the world of dinosaurs and then at midnight everyone goes to bed. But don't be afraid if you hear some strange noises during the night? Maybe it's a dinosaur!

Film

There's also a film about spending a night at the museum. It's called *Night at the Museum* and the actors Ben Stiller and Owen Wilson are in it. This film was in 2006 and in 2009 and 2014 there were two more films with the same actors.

A sleepover

Do you know what a sleepover is? It's when you spend the night at a friend's house, usually with other friends too. It's also called a pyjama party. The Guinness World Record for the biggest sleepover was on 27th September 2014 when 2,400 girls in the north west of England had a pyjama party!

composer someone who writes music

57

Activities

Animals

Can you match the right animals with their festivals?

1. ☐ Crufts
2. ☐ The Royal Welsh Show
3. ☐ Swan Upping
4. ☐ Whittlesey Festival

a swans
b a bear
c dogs
d cows, sheep, horses, pigs and goats

Birthdays

Can you unscramble the words inside the birthday card?

pahyp	tadibyrh	tebs	siwehs	tegsireng
......	......	......	......	......

Customs

▶ 4 **Listen to the text about customs. Are they true (T) or false (F)?**

1. British people drink a lot of tea. ☐
2. 'It's not my cup of tea' means you don't want a drink. ☐
3. British people hate speaking about the weather. ☐
4. British people always smile when they're telling a joke. ☐
5. People are happy if you jump the queue in Britain. ☐

Dance

Answer these questions about dance festivals.

1. What's a Maypole?
2. What's a May Queen?
3. Where was the tallest Maypole?
4. How old is Morris dancing?
5. When did the Industrial Revolution start?

Entertainment

Can you think of the right word?

1　A secret or special power that some people can use
　..................................
2　A woman who is on TV or in a film ....
3　A prize for doing something well ....
4　Something you spend your free time doing ....

Fire

Tell your partner what you remember about one of the fire festivals. Speak for about 2 minutes!

Green Festivals

Complete the sentences.

1　The Chelsea F.................. Show is in May every year.
2　The Green Man Festival is in the Brecon Beacons in W.................. .
3　The Green Gathering uses s.................. energy from the sun.
4　You can see two very big d.................. at the Eden Project.
5　Earthwise 888 is a very g.................. festival.

Heritage

Choose the right answer.

1　There are *13/16* World Heritage Sites in England.
2　People think *a giant/a magician* built the Causeway in Northern Ireland.
3　The Romans built Hadrian's Wall in *122/1222* A.D.
4　Stonehenge is a circle of very tall *trees/stones*.

Islands

Send an email to your friend from one of the Island festivals. Say where you are, what you're doing and what you can see.

Jorvik

Match the sentence with the right place or festival.

1 It's the biggest Viking festival in Europe.
2 It takes place every year in February.
3 It was a very important river port.
4 The Romans built it in 71 A.D.
5 It opened in 1984.
6 A man called Frederick Belmont opened it.

York
Betty's Tea Rooms
Jorvik Museum
Jorvik Festival

Kids

Complete with the right word.

days • making • young • speak • started

The Glasgow film festival .... in 2008 and happens every February in Glasgow in Scotland. It lasts 10 .... It's a festival for .... people from 3-17 years old. They learn about .... films. There are also famous actors who .... at the festival.

Literature

Here are some answers about the life of Charles Dickens. Can you write the questions?

1 7th February 1812.
2 9th June 1870.
3 Rochester in the south of England.
4 Every year in June.
5 Oliver Twist, A Christmas Carol, A Tale of Two Cities, David Copperfield.

Music
Do you know their names?

....

Notting Hill
Match the numbers with the right sentence.

1 ☐ 1966
2 ☐ more than 300
3 ☐ 15,000
4 ☐ 3.5 miles
5 ☐ 1950s
6 ☐ 1999

a different costumes
b people came from the West indies to start a new life
c the carnival first started
d the film 'Notting Hill'
e how long the parade is
f food stalls

On New Year's Eve
Write your New Year's Resolutions for the 1st of January.

I'm going to ....
I'm not going to ....
I promise to ....
I'd like to ....

Patron Saints
Correct the wrong information.

1 Saint George is the patron saint of Ireland.
2 He was born in Greece.
3 People say he killed a dinosaur.
4 English people don't go to work or school on St George's day.
5 People wear a white rose on this day.

61

Queen

Can you remember some information about Queen Elizabeth?

Name: .... Children: ....
Born: .... Grandchildren: ....
Married to: .... Became Queen: ....

Races

Words in the snake. How many words can you find?

boatteamscyclingtimehillsparkrunningroyalhorsehats

Test Your Memory

**Can you remember what you read on pages 42-57?
See if you can answer the questions in 2 minutes!**

1 Where's the oldest tennis competition in the world?
2 The Veteran Car Run starts in London. Where does it finish?
3 How fast does the cheese go in the Cooper's Hill Cheese Rolling Festival?
4 Who were the Tolpuddle Martyrs?
5 What do children do at Halloween?
6 What happens on Stir Up Sunday?
7 What can you eat at the hottest festival in Britain?
8 What do you call a sleep after lunch?

Syllabus

Topics
Festivals
Culture and traditions
Places
Music
Sport
Food
Animals
History
Seasons
Free Time

Notions and Concepts
Describing places
Describing events
Talking about traditions
Making suggestions
Likes and Dislikes

Other
Adverbs
Adjectives
Prepositions
Comparatives and superlatives
Present simple
Past simple
Present perfect
Gerunds

Teen ELI Readers

Stage 1
Maureen Simpson, *In Search of a Missing Friend*
Charles Dickens, *Oliver Twist*
Geoffrey Chaucer, *Canterbury Tales*
J. Borsbey & R. Swan, *The Boat Race Mystery*
Lucy Maud Montgomery, *Anne of Green Gables*
Mark Twain, *A Connecticut Yankee in King Arthur's Court*
Angela Tomkinson, *Great Friends!*
E. Nesbit, *The Railway Children*

Stage 2
Liz Ferretti, *Dear Diary...*
Angela Tomkinson, *Loving London*
Mark Twain, *The Adventures of Tom Sawyer*
Mary Flagan, *The Egyptian Souvenir*
Maria Luisa Banfi, *A Faraway World*
Frances Hodgson Burnett, *The Secret Garden*
Robert Louis Stevenson, *Treasure Island*
Elizabeth Ferretti, *Adventure at Haydon Point*
William Shakespeare, *The Tempest*
Angela Tomkinson, *Festivals are Fun!*
Michael Lacey Freeman, *Dot to Dot*

Stage 3
Anna Claudia Ramos, *Expedition Brazil*
Charles Dickens, *David Copperfield*
Mary Flagan, *Val's Diary*
Maureen Simpson, *Destination Karminia*
Anonymous, *Robin Hood*
Jack London, *The Call of the Wild*
L. M. Alcott, *Little Women*